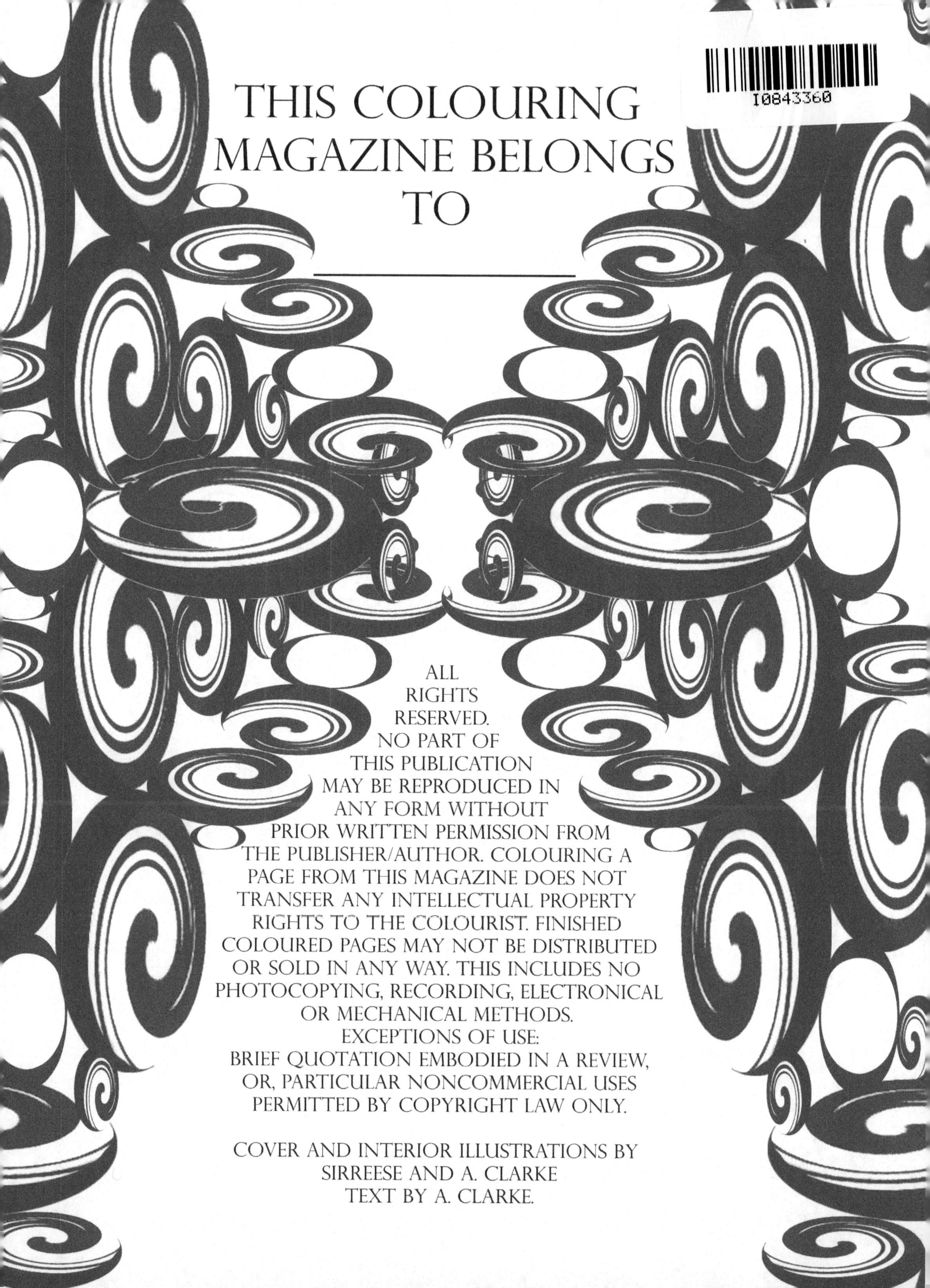

THIS COLOURING MAGAZINE BELONGS TO

____

COVER AND INTERIOR ILLUSTRATIONS BY
SIRREESE AND A. CLARKE
TEXT BY A. CLARKE.

MEET THE RENAISSANCE FEMALES

PARISS
LONDONN
Milann
Angelees

Milann

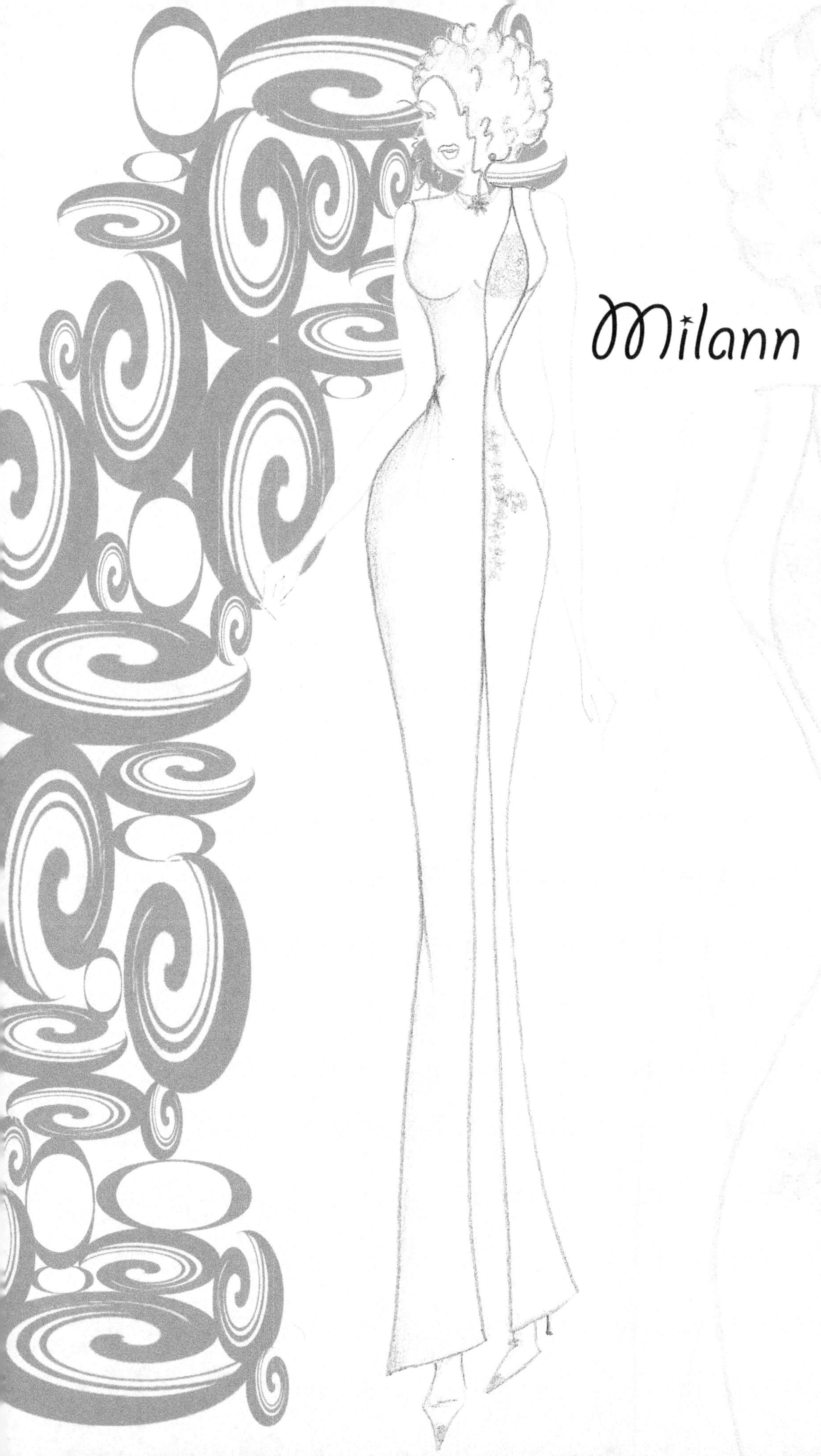

Milann

Milann

Milann

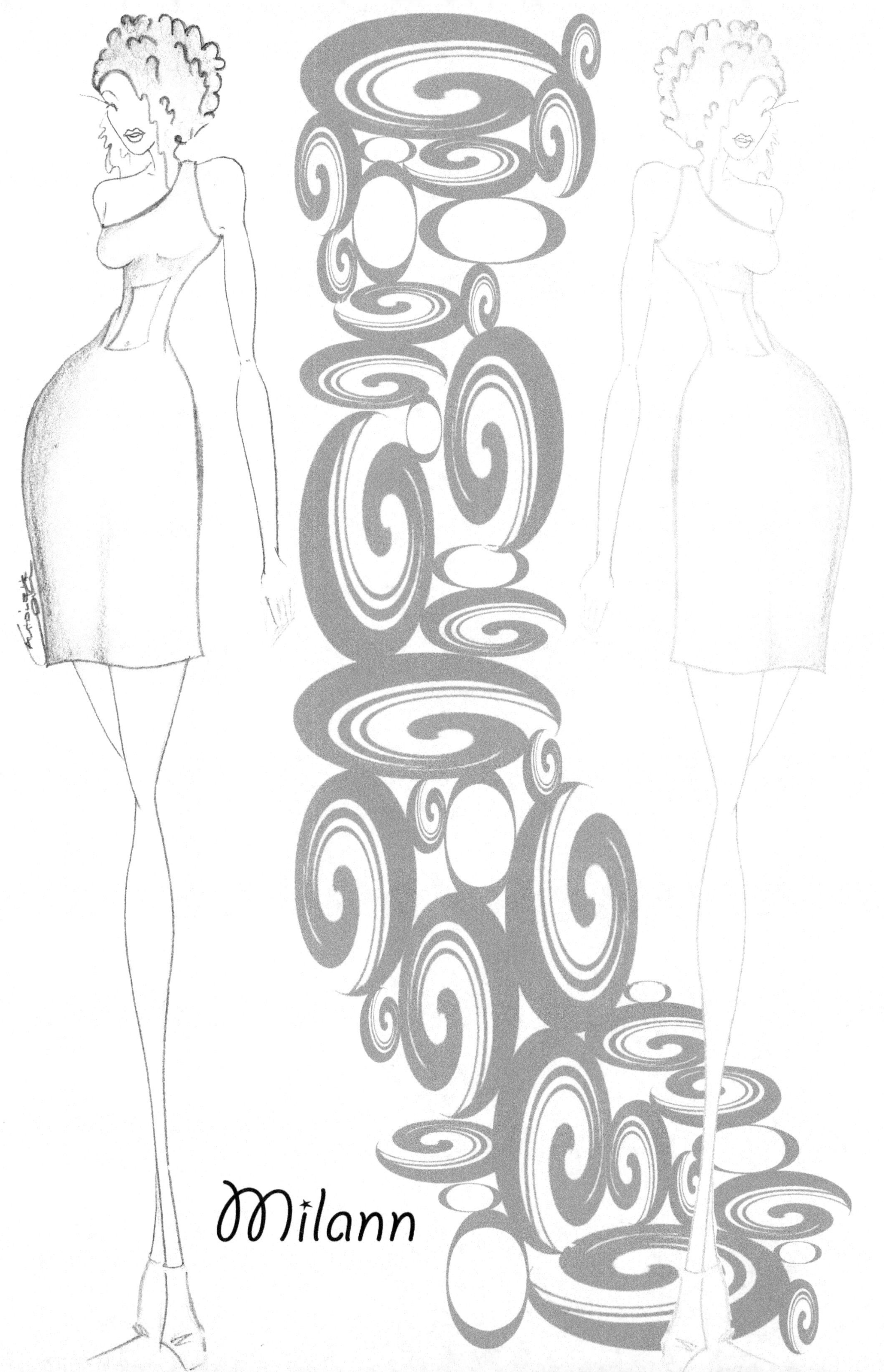

Milann

Milann

Monday	Tuesday	Wednesday	Thursday	Friday	Saturday	Sunday

Plan The Best Week Of Your Life

9

10

11

12

13

14

15

16

17

18

19

20

WWW. SirReese .COM

To Do List

Done

RENAISSANCE FEMALES

PARISS LONDONN Milann Angelees

WWW.SirReese®.COM

RENAISSANCE FEMALES

I AM SPECIAL

You decide who you are and what you are good at...fill in the list

I AM clever

I AM good at what i do

I AM ......

I ....

I CAN ...

I WILL ...

I LIKE ....

I AM ...

WWW. SirReese .COM

Milann

Milann

Milann

Milann

Milann

Milann

SIRREESE®
WWW.SIRREESE.COM